Lett[ing Go]
So You Can
THRIVE!!

The 5-Step Process
That Gets You Unstuck

MOIRA
HUTCHISON

LETTING GO SO YOU CAN THRIVE!
THE 5-STEP PROCESS THAT GETS YOU UNSTUCK

Moira Hutchison

Copyright Notice

Copyright © 2017 Moira Hutchison

This publication is designed to provide accurate and authoritative information in regard to the subject matter covered. It is sold with the understanding that the publisher and author are not thereby engaging in rendering any psychological counselling, or other professional services using this information. If expert advice and assistance are required, the services of a competent qualified licensed professional should be sought.

No part of this publication may be reproduced, stored in a retrieval system or transcribed, in any form or by any means, photocopying, electronic, mechanical recording or otherwise, without prior permission in writing of the author, Attn: Moira Hutchison - Moira@WellnessWithMoira.com

All rights reserved

Table of Contents

Foreword 3
Introduction 5
Chapter 1 – Are You Feeling Stuck? 6
Chapter 2 - Overview of Letting Go as a Pathway to Thriving 10
Chapter 3 – What is Attachment? 13
Chapter 4 - What is Your Attachment Style? 17
Chapter 5 – How to Change Your Attachment Style 22
Chapter 6 - Attachment Versus Connection 25
Chapter 7 – What is Letting Go? 31
Chapter 8 – Balancing Letting Go with Self-Soothing .. 35
Chapter 9 – Letting Go as a Path to Happiness 39
Chapter 10 - Letting Go Versus Forgiving 42
Chapter 11 - Letting Go of Unhealthy Habits 47
Chapter 12 - Your Future Will Find You 52
Chapter 13 - Letting go of Excuses 58
Chapter 14 - Accepting and Allowing 60
Chapter 15 - How to Let Go 65
Chapter 16 – Setting the Stage for the Formula 71
Chapter 17 – The 5-Step Formula for Letting Go 78
Chapter 18 – Aligning to Thrive 90

Chapter 19 – Mastering the Art of Self-Talk 93
Chapter 20 – Finding Your Inspiration........................96
Chapter 21 – Building Your Motivation to Let Go........99
Chapter 22 – What Are Your Next Steps?...................102
About the Author 104

Acknowledgements

My heartfelt gratitude goes to all of my dear friends and acquaintances who encouraged me to write this book – there are far too many of you to mention by name – just know that if we discussed the idea of letting go in order to be the best you can be – I'm referring to you!!

Much love and gratitude to my husband James for his ongoing belief in me and support of the work I do as well as my process of getting where I'm going; and to Jacqueline Richards for writing the foreword.

I am also very grateful to Patrick and Marie Dahdal (and their team!) for having the vision and expertise to bring this project into being.

Most of all I thank all of my clients and students... working with each one of you provides me inner reflection. I really appreciate the feedback you provide about how my work affects your lives – it has been, and continues to be my life purpose, my honour, my inspiration and my reward.

What people are saying about working with Moira:

"Moira's coaching program helped me regain my confidence and helped me figure out what I am most passionate about. I started the program because I was depressed, unemployed, lost and unsure of what career route to take. I was being pulled in different directions and feeling unsure of my skills, abilities and lack of purpose.

Her program offered me tools to help calm my mind, rebuild my confidence, as well as help guide me to my true purpose. Her gentle approach and intuitive abilities offered me the tools and information that I needed to start attracting happiness and prosperity back into my life." ~*Jana*

"Moira has given me an excellent toolbox that helps me deal with life's challenges and difficult relationships. Through her intuitive approach and softness, she promotes self-care. I consider Moira my "soul doctor", because she always makes me feel good about myself." ~*Lynne*

"Moira is highly recommended by me, to anyone who takes seriously their personal development, she helped me find out what it takes most people an entire lifetime to find out about themselves (their purpose)." ~*Karisa*

Foreword

Gratefully, I have come to know Moira through many personal and professional scenarios. As a coach, she discreetly opened up previously unseen doors, and offered teachings for me as I moved through certain life transitions. As a fellow community leader, she created options that revealed both expected and unexpected successful outcomes.

I love the five-part formula that Moira presents and explores herein, and am reminded that you, myself, and Buddha are on the same page as Marianne Williamson's Return to Love states, "When we attach value to things that aren't love—the money, the car, the house, the prestige—we are loving things that can't love us back. We are searching for meaning in the meaningless."

Thank you, Moira, for allowing it all to be unique and applicable to everyone. That is why I chose to endorse this book.

It helped me review my current tool kit, allowing me to see that I was living in a reality hoping for things I thought I needed, and opportunities that I thought were required. My hoping translated into a thriving, but what I was really doing was sinking. You asked us why the "Stinkin' thinking"? Asking the 'Why", led to a couple blessings:

Using the magical number five, Moira guides us to change thoughts, habits, beliefs, ideals and attitudes. It is life changing. My childhood was a challenge and surviving was key... Maybe all kids must go through this? I see many adults still living out their childhood, and this is why each of the five steps of Moira's formula speak to me.

So, I confess: I am attached to Rice Krispy squares. How could I have known there are different kinds of attachments? I thought they only referred to things such as getting married to the forever spouse, or seeking that career with big money and a fantastic title. You had us question if we really need to hold onto absolutely everything...

As we read this wonderful book, we are taught how the Chakras rewire us back to emotional balance. I too see such brilliance in using the chakras to help find ways to get unstuck.

As we look to the future and aspire to thrive alongside you, Moira, LETTING GO SO YOU CAN THRIVE! inspires me to be a messenger, a life lover and a leader.

Moira lays down the rules to be all that you truly can be. Simply to live life from your own space.

Jacqueline Richards RYT, AMP, Author, Speaker, Teacher, and Co-founder Non-Dicloure$ Mastermind

Introduction

For the last ten plus years, I have been investigating the idea of *letting go* through my experiences, reflections, and filters as well as that of my clients, friends, and colleagues. This journey has led me to develop a five-step process which is a powerful foundation to becoming unstuck, engaged in your life and actually thrive.

When I talk about thriving, I think of the dictionary definition - to thrive is to:

1. to prosper; be fortunate or successful.
2. to grow or develop vigorously; flourish.

I don't know about you, but I firmly believe that it is the birthright of everyone in this world to thrive.

In the following chapters, I share my investigations, articles and research into the ideas around feeling stuck; feeling attached or obligated to something or someone in a way that does not feel supportive of you flourishing; and what it is to let go in a graceful, uplifting and healing way.

If you would rather get right into the five-step process, you can jump straight to Chapters 15 – 17. Having said that, I have included a number of other supportive methods and ideas in the preceding chapters which will help you thrive and create all that you wish for and are capable of in this life!

Chapter 1 – Are You Feeling Stuck?

Whenever we get stuck in a rut or when we get off on the wrong path entirely, the universe will use various signs to point this out to us. These are hints that maybe we should take an honest and thorough look at where we are, what we are doing, and what we are going to do about the situation we are in.

Let's look at some signs that you may be experiencing which could indicate that you are stuck and need a different framework to actually feel into the capacity of thriving:

1. *Absolutely everything is tougher and more problematic than it should be.*

    You experience ongoing delays, unexpected problems, etc. Everything you try to do feels like a massive effort.

    Things that should be straightforward to accomplish, are not. You find that you always seem to be in the wrong place at the wrong time. Nothing you do seems to move you forward no matter how hard you try. You feel out of sync with everyone and everything around you.

2. *You feel like you are consistently ending up back in the same situation.*

You work so hard to change things yet the more you try, the more things stay the same. Rather than jumping into something else to try and resolve an issue – perhaps look within to see what it is that has made you feel stuck (sad, angry, irritated, etc.). Once you know what's causing the issue – you can take inspired action rather than recreating the same thing over and over again.

3. *You lack joy and happiness, you feel tired all the time and you lack enthusiasm.*

Deep down you know something is not right. Your heart tells you that you're not in the right place and you're not going in the right direction. You may feel trapped and hopeless. You may start to feel anxious about things and yet not even really aware of why you are feeling the way you do.

4. *You worry about everything.*

You don't trust things to go right and actually with your experiences of late, why would you? You don't have confidence in your decisions, and you have lost touch with your inner self.

5. *Life just feels like it is a constant struggle.*

Physically, emotionally, mentally, and spiritually you just feel drained. You just go through the motions just to make it through the day. You feel like you don't know what to do to get on track with your calling, your sense of meaning.

If any of the five signs listed above describes you, then you need to start taking the time to think about your life, who you truly are and what you want from life. Otherwise, you will remain constantly spinning your wheels stuck in a rut and going nowhere.

People so often try to overcome an obstacle in their life on their own, but then they get discouraged… especially when there doesn't appear to be any real reason for why they can't achieve that success. Sometimes it is just that they need a wee bit of encouragement, a boost or a different perspective to gain the motivation they need to achieve their goals. The truth is: if a person REALLY wanted to do something and could do it on their own - they most likely would have done it already!

One reason that people fall short of their goals is that they keep attempting to solve the same problems with the same toolkit – themselves! How can a toolkit be expected to fix itself?

You're trying to figure out why you keep procrastinating or why you seem to have no motivation to do the things that you KNOW will help you feel better about your life, the pace in which you are moving forward AND the levels of success you can achieve... it seems like no matter how hard you push yourself or how many times you promise yourself that tomorrow will be different, tomorrow you will get it *right*, you end up feeling more and more frustrated with where you are at in life and disappointed with yourself. The solution is the ***Letting Go Process***!

There are many systems, gurus and philosophies out there that promise you a quick fix or great success if you just pay hefty program fees and follow their steps but their approach is never tailored to your unique situation and preferred way of making a change in your life.

You need to learn the ***Letting Go Process*** if you:
- Want to release the frustration and irritation that is keeping you stuck
- Are ready to find out and get into alignment with your ideal health and well-being and/or your true life's calling
- Want to feel better about yourself, about your relationships AND about how you make your living.

Chapter 2 - Overview of Letting Go as a Pathway to Thriving

In preparing to write about the idea of letting go as a healing practice, I reflected upon my own personal life journey as well as witnessing and gathering information from my client's stories and backgrounds. There seems to me to be a direct correlation between the ability of most adult individuals to **let go** in a positive and healthy way and their attachment experiences as a child.

What I have witnessed in my own experience, as well as that of many client case studies, is that to the degree that our natural attachment requirements are met in healthy, highly functioning ways, creates the degree of a foundation of security, confidence, and trust in getting our emotional and mental needs met in healthy and sustainable ways from within.

When we are born into this life, we are conditioned to attach on a physical, emotional and mental way in order to have our needs recognized and met. In fact, other than requiring to be fed, kept warm and safe – we are not aware of what other needs we potentially could have. But we do need to attach psychologically and physically so that we are fed, clothed and nurtured and communicate when we need something attended to and what we need.

The truth is that we do need to depend upon having our emotional and mental needs met from external sources...

it is the best way for our survival in the developmental years because we are on a big learning curve until we mature into capable beings who can think, be and do for ourselves.

It would be great if our lives came with an instruction book – but it doesn't... we need to learn to take responsibility for our life experience as well as what we wish to create and then go forth and do so. This idea brings me to another point – I firmly believe that from a soul perspective, each one of us chooses not only our parents but what era, circumstance and purpose we intend to experience. As souls, before we are born into this physical reality – our connection and interaction happen in a very different way than how we communicate here with words, perceptions (with our five senses) and language.

Back to this idea of choosing our parents – many of you will be shaking your head, thinking, "Wow, if I chose, why did I pick this abusive father or this situation where I was abandoned and left to fend for myself?" Or perhaps you will have some other form of existential-type of questioning spinning around your thought process. The truth of it is that there is some piece of your soul psychology that needed and desired to live through the pain or problem that was caused by these choices.

When you look at the development of your life journey through this type of filter, you may start to understand that those who have abused or caused you pain are those who are the most loving and closely connected to you on a soul level!

OK – I've likely made you throw your hands up in dismay – again! BUT from a soul perspective, no soul wishes to hurt or harm another soul – the true essence of each of us as a soul is pure unconditional love. When you look at life in this light, it helps shift through some layers of toughness, trauma, and pain.

Would you be willing to start to look at the stress, turmoil and pain that you may have experienced in your life up to now as gifts, a catalyst for growth and positive change, and above all as a blessing to you? I realize that this can feel uncomfortable, challenging and perhaps even outlandish to you – especially if you have experienced significant hardship in your life.

Sometimes, in my experience, it has taken many years for me to get to a place of realization that a painful or traumatic experience WAS a blessing and that I did receive gifts, greater insight, and even enlightenment by coming through the situation or event. Sometimes it is quite clear at the outset why I am going through something, and yet other times it is just an education into what I do NOT wish to experience or create.

Chapter 3 – What is Attachment?

It appears that as we came into the 21st century, there has been an ever-increasing sense of isolation and separation or lack of belonging felt by many in this world. The dissatisfaction that happens as a result can be traced to misplaced expectations that society places on external things, other people, and our relationship to these, as the basis for creating happiness in our lives.

The idea that happiness is "out there" or that it's an inbuilt characteristic in some external thing or person pervades our Western consciousness.

Something else that exists is the unrealistic expectation that we can expect and demand that our emotional identity or status and other needs can be met and fulfilled through things, and relationships with others. This attachment to objects or external influences strengthens much of Western thought and beliefs.

The notion of getting one's needs met through a romantic relationship is a recurring theme in the distorted ideals that inspire the Western romantic stereotypes of love and relationship. I believe that it is the seeking to have one's needs met outside oneself that has also led to extensive consumerism, and rising rates of divorce, depression, addictions and perhaps to some degree, even suicide.

The way in which society portrays these biased beliefs through advertising, marketing, persuading and selling in all forms of media, can be described as being an unconscious acting out of what are in fact – unmet universal needs that were blocked, frustrated or denied during the formative years of childhood.

The childhood developmental stages form the basis of the ways in which the later adult will approach and attempt adult relationships. The unmet needs from these childhood stages will show up as behavioral patterns in the adult psyche, waiting for a chance to be expressed through the "inner child" of the adult, by projection, expectation, and demand upon their partner(s).

This impulse forms the basis of the often-misunderstood word "eros" of which the current definition in our society has been degraded to describe a sexual or pornographic depiction, rather than understanding its real basis which is depicted in a meaningful heart and soul connection between two people. Because we are living in physical form, and have evolved from an instinctual basis, these basic drives and instincts will also unconsciously motivate us on occasion to look for heart and soul connection at the physical level through sex or by the intimacy (into-me-see) of sharing ideas, sensations, feelings, and experiences.

I am suggesting here that the way in which the child bonds with its mother will go on to significantly shape the now mature person's ability to approach, enter, maintain and be healthy in adult intimate relationships. This early life developmental phase is one that each one of us had to go through, and which is not often discussed in the conversations concerning letting go, intimacy, adult relationships and romantic love.

We as human beings are only born with limited capacities for self-regulation. We learn and are dependent upon those attachment relationships with our caregivers to give us the context by which we as adults will then have lifelong patterns and tendencies for regulating and reacting to external and internal stimulation in our adult life experience.

Early life disruptions to our process of attachment with parents will have significant consequences for how we as adults will then deal with attachment as adults. These disruptions may show up as a diminished capacity to maintain a sense of self-control and regulation when faced with stimulation from an external or internal source, impairment in developing healthy relationships, and above all – a reduced ability to cope with stress.

Over the last 40 years or so it has been the way of the Western world to witness the breakdown of the traditional family system where the mother was able to stay at home as a choice to be there and raise babies into children at least till they started school. A variety of social, economic and self-actualisation incentives and goals created much of this change.

The increasing demand for raised standards of living and materialistic consumption also created the need for the family system to be supported by incomes of both parents.

These societal and lifestyle choices have not served the early life developmental needs of children. Statistics from many sources are revealing increasing states of learning disabilities in children, anxiety and depressive disorders in school-age children and teenagers, mental health issues and socialization issues. Early life traumas are linked to many of these conditions.

The attachment and bonding process of childhood years is also significant in the subsequent adult ways of finding adult forms of attachment in relationship and intimacy.

Chapter 4 - What is Your Attachment Style?

Our method of attachment affects everything from our partner selection to how well our relationships progress to, sadly, how they end. That is why recognizing our attachment pattern can help us understand our strengths and weaknesses in a relationship.

As we've discussed in the last chapter, an attachment pattern is established in early childhood and continues to function as a working model for relationships in adulthood. This type of attachment influences how each of us reacts to our needs and how we go about getting them met.

When there is a secure attachment pattern, a person is confident and self-assured and can easily interact with others, meeting their needs, as well as another's needs. However, when there is an anxious or avoidant attachment pattern, and a person picks a partner who fits with that maladaptive pattern, she (he) will most likely be choosing someone who isn't the ideal choice to make her (him) happy.

For example, the person with a working model of anxious or preoccupied attachment feels that, to get close to someone and have your needs met, you need to be with your partner all the time and get reassurance. To support this perception of reality, they choose someone who is isolated and hard to connect to. The person with a working model of dismissive or avoidant attachment has the tendency to be distant because their model is that the way to get your needs met is to act like you don't have any. He or she then chooses someone who is more possessive or overly demanding of attention.

In a way, we set ourselves up by finding partners that confirm our models. If we grew up with an insecure attachment pattern, we might project or seek to duplicate similar patterns of relating as adults, even when these patterns hurt us and are not in our best self-interest.

Secure Attachment – Securely attached adults tend to be more satisfied in their relationships. Children with a secure attachment see their parent as a secure base from which they can venture out and independently explore the world. A confident adult has a similar relationship with their romantic partner, feeling safe and connected while allowing themselves and their partner to move freely.

Secure adults offer support when their partner feels distressed. They also go to their partner for comfort when they feel troubled. Their relationship tends to be honest, open and equal, with both people feeling independent, yet loving toward each other.

Secure adults also have a strong sense of self, they feel confident and trust themselves to problem solve and make the best choices for their ultimate good when it comes to career and professional choices.

Anxious-Preoccupied Attachment –Unlike securely attached couples, people with an anxious attachment tend to be desperate to form a fantasy bond. Instead of feeling real love or trust toward their partner, they often feel a sense of an emotional hunger. They are frequently looking for their partner to rescue or complete them. Although they are seeking a sense of safety and security by clinging to their partner, they take actions that pushes their partner away.

Even though anxiously attached individuals act desperate or insecure, more often than not, their behavior exacerbates their fears. When they feel unsure of their partner's feelings and unsafe in their relationship, they often become clingy, demanding or possessive toward their spouse. They may also interpret self-reliant actions by their partner as an affirmation of their fears. For example, if their partner starts socializing more with friends, they may think, "See… He doesn't love me, he is going to leave me, I was right not to trust him."

Dismissive-Avoidant Attachment – People with a dismissive-avoidant attachment have the tendency to distance themselves from their partner emotionally. They may seek isolation and strive to give off the appearance of independence taking on the role of parenting themselves. They often appear to others as being focused on themselves and may be overly attentive to their creature comforts.

This "appearance of independence" is an illusion, as each of us needs a connection on some level. However, people with a dismissive-avoidant attachment tend to lead more inwardly focused lives, both denying the importance of loved ones and detaching easily from them. They are often psychologically defensive and have the ability to shut down emotionally. Even in heated or emotional situations, they can turn off their feelings and not react. For example, if their partner is distressed and threatens to leave them, they would respond by saying, "I don't care."

Fearful-Avoidant Attachment – A person with a fearful avoidant attachment lives in an indecisive state, in which they are afraid of being both too close to or too distant from others. They work hard trying to keep their feelings at bay but are unable to. They can't just avoid their anxiety or run away from their feelings. Instead, they are overwhelmed by their reactions and often experience emotional storms. They tend to be mixed up or unpredictable in their moods.

They see their relationships from the working model that you need to go toward others to get your needs met, but if you get close to others, they will hurt you. In other words, the person they want to go to for safety is the same individual they are frightened to be near. As a result, they have no coordinated strategy for getting their needs met by others.

As adults, these individuals tend to find themselves in rocky or dramatic relationships, with many highs and lows. They often have fears of being abandoned but also struggle with being intimate. They may cling to their partner when they feel rejected, then feel trapped when they are close. Often, the timing seems to be off between them and their partner. A person with fearful avoidant attachment may even wind up in an abusive relationship.

The attachment style you developed as a child based on your relationship with a parent or caretaker doesn't have to define your ways of relating to those you love in your adult life. If you come to know your attachment style, you can uncover ways you are defending yourself from getting close and being emotionally connected and work toward forming an "earned secure connection" in your personal and professional life.

Chapter 5 – How to Change Your Attachment Style

So, once we identify what our attachment style is, what can we do about it? There are a few ways to change your attachment style. The first way is by getting into a long-term relationship with someone who has a healthier attachment style than your own. The second is by making sense of your past through a process of writing an explicit, honest and uncensored description of your early life experience from your perspective.

Writing this clear description helps you better understand how your childhood experiences are still affecting you in your life today. When you create an articulate descriptive of your experience, you rewire your brain to cultivate more security within yourself and your relationships.

The third way to change your attachment style is by engaging in therapy specific to the issue. Therapy helps because appropriate therapy itself offers a secure attachment. In the therapeutic relationship, you ideally feel both safe and seen. As well, therapy can help a person identify the filter they view the world through, challenge their critical inner voices and the defenses they put in place to deal with emotional pain in their earliest relationships.

For example, if you have an anxious, preoccupied attachment style, you can learn to identify and get a hold of your insecurities and moments of anxiety. You can become aware of the critical inner voices that are fueling these feelings and come to recognize the internal working models that are informing your perception of the situation. You can learn techniques to calm down within yourself rather than acting out toward your partner and potentially damaging or harming the relationship. You can start to develop a new image of yourself and trust in others.

Additionally, therapy helps you to do the most valuable thing you can do when it comes to living life free of the more negative burdens of your history; it enables you to create a clear descriptive so that you can both understand your past and evolve in the present.

This process involves both making sense of your story and feeling the full pain of your childhood. Only then, will you truly start to change the lens through which you see the world or the model in which you relate. Instead of unconsciously replicating your childhood, reformulating similar attachments to those you had as a child, you can reshape your relationships to be what you want them to be.

A healthy, secure relationship will further reshape your attachment model, as you have the lived experience of relating to an open, caring, attuned partner. You can begin to see the world in a more realistic light, rather than taking on the point of view of your critical inner voice. You can form healthier relationships and live the life you imagined, not the one prescribed to you from your past.

Chapter 6 - Attachment Versus Connection

As you know, this book is all about *letting go* so you can thrive – as I was researching and developing these ideas, I've given much thought and reflection on the whole idea of attachment. In the previous chapters, we investigated the natural attachment patterns we experience in our formative years.

In Buddhism, teaches that it is our attachment to things that causes our suffering – in other words, our attachment to outcome, personal belongings, our past, and our bodies, anything that is outside of us. Indeed, even our attachment to the idea of *self*.

Anytime you feel suffering you can look at what is causing it and directly trace it to an attachment to something. I do this often, and it does give great insight. For example, is it the loss of a job that causes suffering or the attachment to what the money from that job can bring? Most people who have become unemployed end up better off long term in some way. It doesn't always change the emotional response, but sometimes it helps make it more appropriate to the situation. I see every loss of my past as delivering me into opportunity, of course, at times it takes longer than other times to realize what the opportunity or the blessing is!

Usually, when discussing attachment, someone is bound to ask the question, but what about love? Isn't it a normal human instinct to search for and find love, particularly in the form of relationships and attachment to a partner? And if so, how do we reconcile the idea of non-attachment with the notion of love itself. How can we love and not feel some attachment?

In pondering this question, I have arrived at some conclusions that ring true for me:

Attachment is not what we need to be seeking. It is what we *think* we should look for but what we actually want, as humans with this great capacity for love, is a **connection**. We want to find people to share our true core-selves with who don't run screaming once they hear our darkest thoughts, our past mistakes, our quirks and our dreams. We want people who accept us completely as the incredible spirit we are, not as the fallible human we exist as. We want to be accepted wholeheartedly and fairly as our soul-essence, not our behavior.

What we first need to do is connect to ourselves in this way, forgiving ourselves our faults and striving always to be authentic to the soul-essence we are at the core. In other words, we want to be learning and accepting who we are at all levels of our being and letting it shine for all to see.

The Dalai Lama once said, "Always see the human inside, not their actions." While I'm not perfect, I do look for the spirit inside and try to connect with that rather than attaching myself to how I think a person should behave or has acted in the past. This approach has served me well!

For instance, I know no negative people, I know no bad or evil people. I see good people everywhere I look. I do see misguided choices from places and perspectives I cannot actually understand but accept as true for the person.

Am I just attracting beautiful people or is it I just don't see the bad others see anymore. I don't know – all I know is that I love human beings and believe each and every one of them is, at the core, good.

I know… this all sounds fantastic but what does this look like in real life in a love relationship? Here are a few strange and random questions:

- In your relationship or those you are nurturing, are you focused on getting your love to propose or are you focused on taking care of him or her?
- Are you taking care of him or her to get him to marry you or love you or are you doing it because you love them and value all humans as worthy of love?
- Are you being yourself with them or are you afraid of showing your peculiarities and peccadillos?

- Are you angry at your partner because they didn't pick up their socks or are you smiling because yet again this person you love didn't pick up their socks?
- Are you attached more to the idea of their tidiness than connecting to their heart?
- Are you connected to behavior or are you seeking a real heart to heart connection that transcends all the little attachments to what everyone tells you a relationship ***should*** look like?

Attachment to the idea of what a love relationship should be like is probably why they often fail. What should always be the goal of both partners is to keep the connection. Allowing a person their mistakes, giving them the freedom to come and go and trusting your ability to deal with it if they choose the latter is likely the most important aspect of non-attachment that you can practice. Meanwhile keeping a healthy dose of the same connection to your soul so that you know when behavior is at the extreme and on the unhealthy end of the spectrum. You can love a person and not want to live with their destructive behavior. You can love a person and not want them as part of your life. This is perfectly fine and in fact, an essential part of thriving!

Unconditional love doesn't mean you sacrifice or endanger your well-being for someone who is not capable of returning that love; it means loving them from wherever the safest place for you is. Truth be told, you need to have unconditional love for yourself as well. Perhaps you are connected with someone whose lifestyle isn't something you can live with. Or maybe they are violent or controlling or addicted to something?

Are you attached to the idea that you must live in the same home with the person you love having them actively in your life? Perhaps you can be happy with an alternative arrangement and maintain connection more easily without the trappings of domesticity getting in the way.

Without that connection, is it still possible to be happy in an exclusive love relationship with someone? Yes, you will be able to get along but don't be surprised if eventually, the desire for that connection becomes intense. It is often like hunger and almost as strong as the urge for food. You may not die without it but you may feel you can't fully live. Ideally, you reconnect. But that takes two, and if you don't, it may be time to decide how relevant to your life this connection is.

You can fill the need for that sense of connection with friends and family and work and fun, but still, the desire to connect with that particular person who gets you on every level is intense. It is certainly possible to live a completely fulfilled life without it. I've known many happy single individuals who aren't looking for it. That is not what I'm saying.

What I'm saying is, if this is who you are, and this connection is important to you, beware not to drive it away with attachment to the trappings that society sets down as the norm. So, when it does show up, embrace it but don't attach to it. Let it evolve and allow it be what it is. Enjoy its magic and rejoice in it. Don't make demands on it and it will always evolve into what it's supposed to be for exactly as long as it is supposed to. To be honest, I believe that this applies to each and every other relationship in your life – to your children, your parents, your friends without the burden of expectation. It changes how you interact with people and how they relate to you and is for the best on all levels.

Detach and connect. Give unconditional love – to all humanity and yourself. The love and connection you are looking for will find you. All we need to do is to look for the heart in people, and we will stay on a path that truly allows us to thrive.

Chapter 7 – What is Letting Go?

Sometimes the hardest thing to do in our spiritual lives is let go. So many chains can burden us and then we drag them around with us throughout our life. These might be attached to the heaviest, most cumbersome loads and yet we trudge on, struggling against our very own true nature most of the time, usually because we just do not know how to, or we are afraid of, letting go.

Sometimes we come to recognize our burdens and baggage and sometimes - we cherish them, hoping that others will feel pity for the great weight we carry, or in some way, will respect us more. And yet other times we just don't know any better.

Can you imagine anything dafter than all of this?

We are trying to travel our best journey in our spiritual lives, and yet our path and progress are hampered by our selves insisting upon dragging around these massive weights. Do you know what these chains and burdens are for you?

Is there someone that irritates you or that you dislike? Perhaps even someone that you hate? Is there someone that you have not forgiven? Maybe someone that you cannot forgive? These are all massive weights that we burden our hearts with, scarring them. They are perversions to the perfect unconditional love we each have at our core.

These impurities drag our love down. In fact, they pull our love into common, conditional expressions. We will not be the first to apologize or the first to extend a hand because it is 'their fault' or 'they started it.' We will not be the first to forgive, because 'they do not deserve it.' 'I will not love him until he loves me, and if he stops loving me then I cannot love him.'

What a heaviness we can carry!!

Are there things in your past you wish you had done better? Or other things you'd like you had not done at all? Do you have a cupboard full of 'if-onlys' that haunt you? Do you think about your past or your current situation and have regrets? These are large, heavy anchors that we drag around with us. They stop us from gaining any traction in our spiritual evolution; they lessen our ability to grow and develop and above all, they dim our light.

Do you worry too much? Do you lie in bed worrying? Thinking about whether you have done the right thing, or paid your bills, or what you will do tomorrow and 'if only' this or that. All these are chains. Burdens.

Let them go – release them once and for good!

Forgive anyone and everyone who may have wronged you in any way. This is not for their benefit – it is for YOU. The hate or the grudge that you carry around is a noose around your neck, not theirs. It is contributing to your tension, making you feel stressed and irritated - let it go! Open yourself to the highest love of all, the love that is without condition or expectation of love in return.

Forget your 'if-onlys' - let them go. Regret helps no one. Just decide to let go of the things you can't control and take ownership of the things you can. You cannot control all the events of your life, but you can control your state of mind during them. It is your state of mind that determines your happiness, not the events of your life. You are the master of your happiness because you are the master of your state of mind - take control.

Finally, don't worry, be happy! (Do you feel a bit of reggae coming on?) Worry is a burdensome mental disease that only you can heal. It is a looping program, a virus for your spiritual life - let it go - let it all go. Do all you can to deal with your worries now! No procrastination. Just deal with them and then LET THEM GO!

Our time is now at this moment. Our power is the infinite paradise within us. Our future is held within the realization of our highest and best way of being, anything that detracts from that are burdens.

Here is an exercise for you to access your Inner Voice:

Sit with your eyes closed and concentrate all of your attention on your heart. Repeat to yourself 2-3 times "I am not my body, I am not my mind - I am my soul."

This is your true reality.

This is the real nature of you – your inner voice. Your conscience that has spoken to you since the beginning of you – this is the real you. For a moment, reflect upon the possibility that the thinking, physical feeling being that we think of as ourselves is not the real us, but that tiny, silent little voice within is the *real* us. That tiny little voice that tries to prompt us tries to guide us and we tend to ignore, is our highest reality.

That soft, gentle inner voice that we ignore day in and day out is what we are trying to grow into. That is our highest self!! Will you start to listen, to pay attention more? Is that possible for you?

Listen very quietly and hear what your inner voice has to say – listen to the answer it has for you. Is that the voice of your soul? Focus all of your attention on it and let everything else go. Let everything else go. Sit still and silent and focus your entire life past, present and future on your soul and listen. Listen with all your heart... It is your own eternal and infinite voice.

Chapter 8 – Balancing Letting Go with Self-Soothing

When doing the inner work required to meet with and then let go of the beliefs, thoughts, and habits that are blocking you from being fully you on all levels of your being, it is important to have some tools to help shift through the process. Self-soothing is an skill essential for emotional and physical well-being.

Many of us, particularly those who are emotionally sensitive, either forget or just do not know about the importance of self-soothing activities. In moments of upset or of feeling triggered, it can be difficult to think about calming yourself. Plus, self-soothing does not come naturally to everyone, and it does require some thought and action.

A stress response is a natural part of our survival pattern. The amygdala is known to be the part of your brain that processes underlying feelings. The amygdala plays a significant role in sounding an alert for threatening situations and triggers the fight or flight behaviors. This works well when there truly is a threat that you need to run away from or defend yourself against. Otherwise, your body suffers from being on high alert when it doesn't need that reaction.

Feeling threatened when you are not is unpleasant and exhausting. People who have suffered traumatic experiences may find they are easily stressed and often are in the flight or fight state when there is no current danger. In addition to being a part of our threat alert system, the amygdala also seems to be involved in emotional memories.

Creating sensations that instill the reality that there is no emergency helps calm the body's alert system so the brain (actually, the prefrontal cortex) can regain its ability to think and plan. If you are sipping hot tea wrapped in a soft blanket or lazing in a bubble bath, then there must be no reason to run at full speed to the nearest cave!

Whatever the reason or origin of the emotional sensitivity, self-soothing can help. Self-soothing is part of finding a middle ground, a gray area, between being detached or numb and experiencing an emotional crisis or upheaval. Allowing yourself to experience the uncomfortable emotions (without feeding them and making them more intense) enables the feelings to pass. Soothing yourself helps you accept the experience without acting in ways that are not helpful in the long run, or blocking the emotions, which makes the emotions become larger or be expressed in ways you didn't intend.

What Are YOUR Self-Soothing Activities?
Usually, soothing activities are related to the senses. Different people are comforted in different ways and may prefer one sense over another. Sometimes what is

soothing for one situation is not the same as what is soothing in a different situation.

When your alert system is firing danger, then physical activity may help, like playing a fast-moving game of racquetball or going for a brisk walk.

When the upset is more about feeling hurt or sad, activities such as sipping hot tea or petting a pet may be more nurturing. The smell of apple pie baking, a beautiful sunset, the softness of a cat's fur, the sound of birds singing, the taste of chocolate or the sensation of rocking. Reading a good book can be soothing for some. Being with a good friend, someone you feel safe with and loved by, can be soothing.

Some may feel soothed by focusing on a specific sense. Some people are more visual than others and some are more auditory. Experiment with the different senses to see what works best for you. You may want to create a self-soothing box full of options that you know are effective for you. When you are upset, searching for a particular song or even remembering what is soothing is hard. Put a list of your self-soothing activities in the box together with some of the objects you might need.

Create Self-Soothing Experiences
A self-soothing experience involves more than one sense and provides an overall feel of valuing the self. Having your favorite meal at a table set with cloth napkins and beautiful dishes while listening to music you love would

be a self-soothing experience for some. A bubble bath with your favorite scent, a favorite drink, and listening to a book on tape could also be a self-soothing experience.

More Self-Soothing Activities
Performing an act of kindness for others can be soothing, particularly if you are feeling disappointed in yourself. Often helping those who are less fortunate is useful in that situation too. Accomplishing tasks such as cleaning your house or organizing your closet can help with uncomfortable feelings. Writing, playing, and laughing can all be soothing by helping you detach and feel more in control of your emotional experience.

Focusing on your sense of meaning may be soothing. This meaning might be about knowing your purpose in life, or it might be about a spiritual connection. Focusing on what is truly important to you can help you let the less important go. Perhaps you could consider meditation or prayer.

Finding out what works best for you through practicing self-soothing in different situations will help you manage your emotions more effectively. You may want a way of reminding yourself to self-soothe and what to do because we do not think clearly when upset. Motivation to self-calm in tense moments can be kind of low on the priority list!!

Chapter 9 – Letting Go as a Path to Happiness

The road to health and happiness is often not a way of adding to something, but more of a removal or a letting go. This is an important principle of healing that is not often discussed.

The media, books and the society in which we live in the Western world often encourage us to obtain more, to attain great heights, to grow and accumulate degrees, things, friends, children, money and so on. Of course, all of this has its place. However, the opposite – learning to let go of the past, in particular, and of any and all attitudes, beliefs, emotions, things, friends and other "baggage" that are holding us back - is often a hidden key to happiness and healing. It is an essential component to making room for more beautiful things to come. Let's further explore the secret of the very freeing process of letting go.

So - What's Involved in "Letting Go"?
It's all about leaving your comfort zone. Learning to let go of old habits, ideas, people who are not serving your best interests, and much more – it is not always an easy task, but the benefits are completely worth the effort! The main reason is that one must leave one's comfort zone or everyday situations, habits and thinking patterns. This can be stressful, sometimes to the extreme. Therefore, many people simply do not do it. They make

excuse after excuse as to why they should or could not change, rather than embrace change. This is the main stumbling block for many people when it comes to letting go of anything in their life.

Letting go can be as simple as recycling or giving away old clothing. It can be as radical as leaving a long-standing marriage or friendship and changing one's entire lifestyle. Whatever it is, it is always going to be somewhat painful. I mention this because the feeling of loss that accompanies any letting go is perfectly normal, and should not be confused or ignored. If one expects no pain, then when the pain of separation and letting go and abandonment sets in, many people turn and run away rather than step forward boldly. This is often the main reason that most people do not make the most of their lives.

Letting go is always somewhat scary. Letting go is also frightening for other reasons. One is that the future is always unknown. The past, as miserable as it may have been, is known and therefore one can more easily navigate through it, knowing at least what to expect, even if it is not that great. The future, however, is entirely unknown and this is very unnerving for most people. This is the second important stumbling block that prevents most people from moving forward in their lives.

The third block is that the future is unpredictable. This is related to the second block but is somewhat different. It means that no matter how well you plan ahead, the future is inherently difficult to prepare for, unlike past attitudes, relationships and habits with which one is more familiar. This also stops some people from moving on because they don't even know what they need to prepare for their futures.

The fourth block is that few people realize that when one actually lets go and continues forward, one will have few if any reference points to evaluate their next move. This may seem corny, but is vital in the processes of developing into the grandest version of YOU!

Another block to movement or moving on in your life is thinking you will lose some essential part of your identity, personality, friendships, family relations or other parts of yourself that you value. To be honest, this has been a stumbling block for me at times too. Know that if you truly embrace your future, this will not happen. In fact, when you move ahead and let go of your past, more, not less of your personality and gifts will manifest.

I can only tell you this from experience, and everyone experiences this fear that they will lose their identity, talents, and friendships, etc. You may seem to lose some, but if you do then anything you lose was not you. This may sound harsh, but many of us do not actually know our deepest self, our deepest identity, and even who our real friends are.

Chapter 10 - Letting Go Versus Forgiving

These two concepts are quite similar if one forgives completely. However, it is possible to let go of something or someone without forgiving. It is not feasible to forgive completely without letting go.

Many clients have asked me about the ideas of forgiveness, acceptance and letting go and it does appear that this can be somewhat of a gray area for some people to know what each is and what it means to forgive, to let go or to accept. As this is such an important topic for our physical, emotional, mental and spiritual health - I thought it would be of benefit to explore the fundamental differences.

Something that many people struggle with, perhaps something you struggle with too, is forgiving others when they have hurt you. People can be very hurtful with their words or their actions, and we can be very susceptible to being wounded in this way. Especially as children, we were vulnerable to all of the adults around us, you have no power, no control, no say and you could have often been at the mercy of an adult's anger or frustration. As an adult, you are still often just as fragile to hurts, you just learn to cover it up with a mask as you can't walk around crying or yelling or being upset all of the time nor do you want to show people your reactions.

As an adult, it is important to learn forgiveness because - not to forgive has adverse consequences for you and your overall health and sense of well-being. Not forgiving creates turmoil and negative emotional and mental states, it can cause physical ailments and creates disharmony in your energetic system. It affects how you live your life, the experiences you have (and don't have) as well as the type of people you attract into your experience.

This is a problem. Individuals who don't forgive end up being bitter, resentful and cynical about life and they often have an endless list of things that they are angry about or things that haven't worked out for them or people who have done them wrong. They end up blaming life for what has happened to them and shut off to the many wonderful experiences life has to offer to those with an open heart.

Now that I have said all of this – it is important to remember that forgiveness does not mean acceptance. It never means saying what happened to you is okay, or that it was acceptable that someone hurt you. This is where people often get confused. You forgive someone for *you*, not for the other person. You forgive them because you don't want to get sick or have that resentment clouding up your life. It ends up being you walking around angry or sad at the person who hurt you; it ends up hurting you. The other person may have no idea at all, or they may not care what has happened, so it often doesn't affect them at all. So this is why you must do it for you and you alone.

Acceptance is more about accepting the fact that it happened. You cannot turn back time; you cannot change things that occurred in the past, all you can do is accept that it did happen and see what you could learn from it and what was the gift from the experience. It can be challenging to learn from negative and painful experiences, but there is always something that comes out of it that you can feel gratitude for. The negative experiences I have had throughout my life have helped to develop me into the therapist I am today.

For sure, without those experiences, I may have suffered less pain, but I also would not have grown as a result and would not have gone on my journey of self-discovery and then going on to help others. For me learning about myself and connecting to my happiness and fulfillment has been the most amazing thing I have done in my life and will continue to be... we do this through suffering. Without suffering, we would have no reason to seek to know ourselves, know Spirit, (Source, the Divine, God, Allah - you fill in the blank etc.) know others, know the universe and so on.

Letting go is where you should end up at the end of the forgiveness process. You let go of any attachment to negativity about the event, to resentment about the event and to the event itself. You don't hold a charge on the event anymore. In other words, you can think about it without getting overly emotional or having a significant triggered reaction. You can think and talk about it like you were telling a story about someone else because you have healed it; not because you are detached from it or numb to it.

I am not saying this is easy and it can only happen when you have processed out the feelings of hurt and let go of blame. It can take many years to do this depending on the situation and how bad the damage is. But it is possible for everyone to achieve this if that is what they want. Retracting blame is the biggest and hardest step so once you have done that everything is easier from there and you will feel better about yourself just from that step.

When you take back blame from people and life, you can start to see things with a new perspective and realize why others act as they do. Sometimes, when stuck in our pain we don't see just how damaged the other person is and that they are incapable of loving you or treating you in the way you want and need due to their unresolved issues. Most people don't hurt others intentionally (only psychopaths and sociopaths do that), but it can sometimes appear that way. More often than not, they are just doing the best they can with what they had at the time. This doesn't excuse their behavior, but it can help you understand where they were coming from.

Resolving something in yourself and deciding to forgive someone and let it go doesn't mean you have to tell that person you forgive them either. As I said, you do it for you, so you aren't damaged by holding negativity for extended periods of time. Forgiveness is an inner process, something you do inside yourself and if you choose you can reach out to forgive someone if you want that relationship back in your life. Otherwise, you can just wish that person well silently and opt not to have them in your life. As long as there are no hard feelings, in the end, that's what matters to you.

Chapter 11 - Letting Go of Unhealthy Habits

Dysfunctional patterns offer temporary relief, but they add stress and strain in the long run. These practices may include things like - staying up later than 10:30 or 11:00 p.m., taking on too many obligations, distracting oneself or procrastinating instead of facing challenges at work, or perhaps even avoiding exercise. Other unhealthy habits include eating too much, skipping meals, drinking too much coffee or alcohol, smoking, eating junk food or sugar, getting upset over trivial issues or taking stimulants or depressants instead of addressing the deeper causes of unhappiness.

To let go of any of these habits, it first requires a commitment to yourself. You *are* worth the effort! Often, a good solution is to institute better practices. For example, instead of staying up late, record the late television show, drink a mug of calming herbal tea to help you slow down and relax, decide you will not start projects after dinnertime, and start preparing for bed early.

Obligations: To avoid accepting too many commitments, set aside time periods on your calendar each day that is just for you - for meals, exercise, a long walk by yourself, a bath, perhaps, or maybe another favorite past-time or activity. Refuse to give up these time slots for anyone or anything. You may feel selfish, or maybe you will miss parties or other gatherings, but it is all good practice to ensure that you create and maintain optimal levels of happiness and calmness in your life... and that in itself is the best gift you can give to yourself, your loved ones and everyone who you come into contact with.

In particular, set aside time for rest, to breathe deeply, to relax and to have peaceful, sit-down meals. This also means setting aside enough time to shop for food and to prepare meals with love. Eating is not something to squeeze in between appointments. Especially avoid eating in your car, or while conducting business at an office. Establishing these simple habits will influence all your other patterns in many cases. Good habits spawn other healthy habits, in other words. The rewards in your health will more than compensate for the time taken to focus on these simple healthy habits.

If you tend to overdo alcohol, coffee, sugar, junk food or medications, there are many ways to shift your habits. Getting enough rest and sleep, eating better and exercising regularly in a gentle and mild way will assist in reducing cravings. Don't keep tempting foods, beverages or drugs in your space. Ask for cooperation from those around you. Keep better quality foods on hand at all times for when temptation arises. Experiment with alternatives. Sometimes a support group and professional help are also excellent.

When you try to change any habit, I encourage you to do so in the spirit of celebration, not from need. The spirit of celebration means that you have already overcome it in your mind. You just need a wee bit of help to work out the details! This is a far cry from feeling like you are a victim of some habit and that someone or some therapy is needed to "fix" you.

Another trick for letting go of unwanted habits is to regularly treat yourself to healthy activities and therapies that balance and enhance mind and body. These can include Reiki, other forms of energy work, EFT (Emotion Freedom Technique) tapping, reflexology treatments, massage, chiropractic adjustments and maybe a class of gentle yoga, tai chi or something similar.
Some other more general suggestions to help you let go of the past are to seek balance and harmony in every aspect of your life. If someone or something is continually knocking you out of balance, look at it carefully.

Try on an ongoing basis to separate the important from the unimportant, the essential from the non-essential. This is an ancient teaching that is critical today. Is hanging out with your friends necessary? The answer is usually no. Is eating correctly and sleeping plenty each night essential? The answer is a definite yes if you want to be healthy.

It is also very helpful to live in a clean, safe and quiet location, surrounded by some of nature's beauty. It is so much less important is to have a lot of things, a big house, or other "trappings" of society.

Remember always that the body follows the mind. Therefore, try to be aware of what your mind is focused on as much as you can. Note what you focus on, what you think about, and what you tend to ignore. For example, if you focus too much on physical symptoms and conditions, you will often perpetuate them without realizing why this occurs. If instead, you focus on Spirit, on being grateful for whatever you have, no matter how little it is, on helping others rather than on receiving help from others, you will heal so much faster.

Also, of course, focus upon what you can let go of that is in your way. This can be anything from a type of food or habit to a thinking pattern or an attitude or a person. Contrary to many books, for example, families need not "stick together" when the children are grown up, or even before in some cases.

Be careful not to be trapped in popular belief systems that are harmful to you. However, this does not mean throwing out all societal norms, which is another trap for some young people of today.

Physical symptoms: Often physical symptoms are best seen as conversations your body is trying to have with you. This is a much more wholesome and in fact more real understanding of many symptoms, rather than thinking in terms of "diseases" that are out to get you. What are your symptoms telling you? Ask often, and you will get answers, particularly if you allow yourself quiet time to contemplate and meditate every day. Taking a daily walk is a wonderful way to empty your mind, let go of the day's stresses and worries and allow your future to come to you.

Chapter 12 - Your Future Will Find You

This is a great spiritual lesson. I meet so many people who are genuinely caught up by the idea of "finding themselves." This often means finding a career, a relationship, love, power, money or something like this. I have concluded that the key is making room for your future by letting go of your entire past.

I emphasize entire past because for me this is what it takes. In other words, question everything and everyone in your life. Let them all go mentally and emotionally. This does not mean you must get a divorce or leave school, however. It means to be free in your mind. Then you will figure out in an objective way if the job, the school, the friends and so on are really for you. But you must first let them all go emotionally so that you can see where the future may lie. That is the key.

Letting go of Emotions and Beliefs
Views that may need to be let go include many fears, all resentments, guilt, at times, remorse, extreme seriousness, and most judgments expressed as 'shoulds', 'have-tos' 'musts', and 'oughts'.

These familiar buddies have a way of hanging around, changing form in deceptive ways, and then blocking you from your future. Often, we are not even aware of their presence in the dark recesses of the mind.

This is where true friends and even strangers can be extremely helpful, at times. Try to listen to those who are bold enough to speak up to you, saying things that may not feel good to you or them, but which sometimes need to be said. Too often, we shun those who speak the truth to us and only embrace those who think just like us.

Affirmations to help let go of the past: A few carefully chosen and simple statements may also be helpful to dredge up deeply held resentments and negative attitudes. Such declarations are not intended to be used for whitewashing or covering over stuff that needs to be brought up for healing. The purpose of such an affirmation is not to change anything, but just to bring up all thoughts that are unlike the affirmation.

For example, the affirmation, "I choose fearlessness" will accelerate or bring up any and all thoughts of fear within you if you say it often. Try it for a week or two, and you will see this if you do it regularly and with conviction.

Know that in spite of your best efforts to let them go, old belief patterns will often continue to come up for a while, especially if one is in the habit of indulging them. Just denying them usually won't make them go away.

Instead, letting go means to notice them, but don't allow them to take up residence in your mind. Notice them, bless them and see them as a relic of a dead past. Turn them over to a higher power. Take a walk, take a nap or otherwise shift your focus and let them go. You do have a choice which emotions and thoughts you will entertain in your mind. It takes a lot of practice, but the old ideas will begin to lose their hold on you.

For negative thoughts: Try entertaining positive thoughts instead, such as that only love is real and I am the expression of love in this world of form. Just try these ideas on for size. At first, they may seem outlandish, however, with practice, they become more comfortable and realistic. Eventually, you will wonder why you believed otherwise for so many years.

If friends or family continually remind you of the old fears and anger, it is fine to tell them thanks, but you are not interested anymore. It is alright to say you have decided to be that which you would pass onto others. You figured out that anger and fear heal nothing, and only hurt the one who holds onto them. In letting go of judgments about others, it may help to realize that we don't often see the big picture, and we don't know what is best for others.

Doubt and question the negatives in your life and your mind. If you cannot embrace a positive thought to replace a negative thought or emotion, at least doubt the negative. This is a helpful technique that helped me turn around a lot of negative thinking and feeling... Each time I found myself thinking negatively, I would doubt myself purposely. I would think and say, "But maybe I'm wrong about that." This is a way to intentionally confuse the negative part of yourself, which in turn weakens it drastically. Before, you most likely doubted the positive aspects of your life or yourself. Why not start to question the negative aspects as well!

Stay in the present moment: As you explore letting go, it can often help to remember that "I am in the right place at the right time." This statement can help counteract one way that your mind keeps you in old beliefs and attitudes. It does this by reminding you of something in your past that is familiar and reinforces your old beliefs and thoughts. Realize that your past was perfect, but it is time to move on, let it go completely so that your future can come to you.

Do not compare yourself to other people. Comparing always leads to unhappiness. You will learn that there will always be someone more beautiful, smarter, more successful, "happier," etc. Later, as you embrace your future completely, you will realize that comparing yourself with others, for the most part, is a complete waste of time. You are not that person, and your life should look entirely different from that of others. If it is a carbon copy of your neighbors, you are most likely not living your life, but merely "keeping up with Jones's."

Instead, how about trying to set a new example. Try to be one who inspires others. Show up as you wish others to be. Be a friend, rather than look for a friend. Be a good partner, business person, student, etc. It is so much more fun and productive than comparing yourself or trying to make everyone and everything else conform to your desires.

Letting go also applies to the jaded fear-based and ego-based voices that often whisper in our ears, and serve only to confuse and hold us back. Identifying these false voices and learning to ignore them gets easier with practice.

Letting go may involve questioning every belief system you have ever been taught. Ask yourself, is this belief in alignment with the reality that I am loved by the Universe (Creator / God / Allah / etc.) infinitely more than I can imagine?

I implore you... do not rebel just for rebellion's sake. Rebelling is not at all the same as letting go of the past. Rebellion is a very popular activity in this day and age that often wastes years of people's lives. They think they are running toward their future, but are just running away from their past!

Letting go does not just propel you in any other direction. It is just a total and repeated emptying of the mind and the emotions so that something else can come in and show you your way.

If you find yourself rebelling, take a deep breath, slow down and just allow yourself to question and allow the answers to be revealed.

Have you heard of the concepts of 'you get what you focus on', or - 'ask and you shall receive', or - 'you reap what you sow,' or even - 'what you resist persists'? These simple statements are as true today as they were when first written. Many people do want to let go, but they do not ask (or stop resisting) frequently enough. This is an important concept to keep in mind. For example, many seek more friends, success, money, or health. If they could reframe this seeking and focus more on the letting go of the past, which is often the reason for their trouble and seeming failures, they might find that a greater sense of grace, ease, and abundance settles into their lives.

Chapter 13 - Letting go of Excuses

Excuses rob you of your personal power - take a deep breath and let this thought percolate deeply for you. An excuse tends to imply that you were a victim of circumstances and therefore you are powerless and not responsible for your actions. They may make you seem more innocent, but in reality, they just dis-empower you.

The opposite of making excuses is to take complete and total responsibility for your life. The main reason for taking responsibility is that it is so awesomely empowering! It implies correctly that if things are a mess, you have the power to change them, whereas if you make excuses, the implication is you are a victim and not nearly as capable of changing your life. The circumstances of our life are intended to be our playground, not our overlord or dictator.

I encourage you to try on the idea of taking full responsibility for everything in your life, even the negatives as you perceive them, such as alcoholic parents, mean partners, troublesome children, horrible ailments or other seeming turmoil, strife and misfortunes.

Taking full responsibility may seem overwhelming, but it is not so at all. It is a new way in which to live that prepares you for an enjoyable and fulfilling future full of joy, peace, and love.

What's Possible When You Let Go of 'Stinking Thinking'?

Where you find yourself at this present moment is the result of your past thoughts, attitudes, and actions to a much greater extent than you might imagine. Practicing and living the 'letting go' philosophy each day will develop into amazing life changes - sometimes very quickly. Many types of problems can improve, and life becomes much simpler and happier. Why is this? You may ask... It's because it was the old thoughts and attitudes that created the problems in the first place.

Change your thoughts, habits, beliefs, ideals and attitudes, and over time your entire life will change. The amazing changes that happen can sometimes be hard to believe.

Chapter 14 - Accepting and Allowing

Something that is vital in this discussion about letting go is for you to accept ALL of the love of the Universe (Creator / God / Allah / etc.) for you into your life. This can sometimes feel like the hardest thing in the world to do. We become so used to struggling and straining to get what we want that the idea of just allowing and accepting seems somewhat outlandish and challenging.

Allowing and accepting are in fact a large part of letting go. You see, holding on to the past is like living on autopilot, even though most people think they are in control and "creating their future." Most are not. They are merely continuing to live out their prior beliefs and ideas in new forms.

Once you have set your intention to let go of your entire past, the next logical and related step is to relax and allow and accept the new beliefs and principles into your life. This will happen automatically as you make room for them and search honestly.

Did you know that grace is your birthright? It is not dependent on what you do or what you are. It is undeserved and unearned. It is like the sun that shines on everyone equally, regardless of their past thoughts and past behaviors.

Allowing and accepting may be unfamiliar words, and even less familiar ways of living. Living with ease and by grace works, often much better than the old way of struggle and striving.

Choosing Peace

Another aspect of letting go that is also often overlooked is a decision that must accompany the ***letting go process***. This is to choose to be at peace within consciously. Since this can seem a wee bit complex, I want to explain it carefully. First, let's dig a bit deeper into this:

It means a deliberate choice to be at peace all of the time, not just when things are going well, and life is fun. Also, it means choosing for peace even if it hurts – and it will hurt at times (sorry!!).

For example, it can mean giving up the sweet feeling of revenge against friends and others who appear to slight you or harm you. It can mean walking away from a situation in which you could choose to fight back. Of course, there are times when fighting is the correct response, but it must be done from a place of peace within. This is the key, and it is not an easy thing to understand. In other words, it must come from within. It is not about gritting your teeth and walking away, or putting on a happy smile while you fume underneath. One can fight a fair fight without anger and resentment. That is the idea here.

Now let us investigate further about what choosing for peace within does not mean. It does not mean denying your anger, fear or upset. It means observing your feelings, expressing them when appropriate, and then letting them go.

It also does not mean being a doormat or avoiding confrontation. It means learning how to communicate effectively and acting boldly, at times, but not from anger.

This attitude may take some time to cultivate, but is a truly beautiful way to live.

A phrase to practice is "I can be at peace with this" (no matter what 'this' is). It is possible to be at peace even in the midst of chaos and turmoil. There are many stories of people who achieve this feat. Of the finest, two that are somewhat familiar are the stories of George Washington and Abraham Lincoln in American history. These men were surrounded by chaos, horror, intrigue, and terrible living conditions. They remained calm, and as a result inspired the nation.

Always recall that this kind of peace within, or your lack thereof, always affects those around you. When you choose peace within, others see that they too have this choice. This is a wonderful gift to your children and others around you. However, if you continue to be caught up in external events and tied to your past traumas, anger, and resentments, you will keep those around you somewhat caught up as well. Keep this in mind, as it is a key to family peace and relationship success.

Be the model, in other words, rather than waiting for others to let go of their past and treat you as you wish to be treated.

Friends and Relationships

Relationships will change drastically as you let go of your past. This is inevitable and not to be feared. As you change, those around you must see you differently. Some will like what they see, but others will not. A lot of courage is required in this area – if you do not push through you will be showing yourself that you are not willing to let go of the past.

This is a delicate area, I realize, especially in this day of easy divorce and little loyalty among many families and friends. Divorce should always be thought out carefully. Leaving friends or family can be an easy way out and a substitute for examining old, dark patterns of thought and behavior that lead to discord and disharmony. While many friendships are not the best, our instant-gratification, throw-away culture is certainly not the answer, either.

Let go of those who dishonor you. On the other hand, when "friends," family members or partners dishonor you by dishonoring their contracts and agreements with you, be prepared to take vigorous action. Otherwise, you dishonor yourself.

Some people refuse to take responsibility for themselves and insist that you take responsibility for their happiness. They may be committed to unhappiness or anger. At these times, the most loving action may be to recall that all who love are joined at the level of the mind, but that physical separation is sometimes needed.

In other cases, another may not dishonor you, but you may realize that your focus or level of living is different from theirs. It is not a judgment, just an observation. Staying with them may mean you must stay at or near their level, which can cause depression and illness in a sensitive person.

With great compassion, you may realize you cannot maintain your integrity and keep living as another person would wish, although it may seem perfectly acceptable to outsiders. Each situation is different. As with any important decision, go within and ask for guidance and you will receive it.

One key thing is to recall that letting go of the past is first and foremost about emotionally and mentally letting go, not physically letting go. It is about stopping your emotional investment in other people and things so that you can see clearly. Then the right course of action will often become apparent to you without emotional overtones.

Chapter 15 - How to Let Go

When you are holding something in your hands that you don't want to hold on to anymore, what do you do? You let it go!

If it is a hot pan that is burning your hand, you let go quickly. You drop it and don't care where it lands just as long as it is away from you and not near anyone else, either. To keep holding it would be absurd; You don't hold on to something that's so painful.

Of course, maybe you wanted that rice you were cooking, and maybe it's going to land on the floor and be inedible – but you don't care. You know the longer you hold the flesh-burning pan, the more damage it will do to you. You must let go now and deal with the mess later. You must let go and treat the burn right away and minimize the impact of the injury. It is the smart thing to do.

So, what's the first step to letting go? You notice the pain… you feel the pain. It is evident that something is wrong. In the case of the hot pan, your response to letting go is as quick as a flash. You understand that no good will come from clinging on to it. In fact, you know that continuing to grasp on to it will only make the situation worse.

But what about other things that are hurting you – how do you let go? The first step to letting go of anything is the same: you notice the pain… you feel the pain. You feel that something is wrong. Then, you make a decision: Do I want to continue to feel this pain or do I want to let it go?

The stronger the pain you are feeling, the more confident you can be that what's wrong will not go away of its own accord. You must respond in some way.

Now, let's put this into a context that everyone can relate to because I truly believe we all hold on to things that are not good for us at some point in our lives.

Here are some of the things I've clung to when I should have let go:

- I held on to the wish that a career situation in my past could have been different.
- I held on to an image of how a particular relationship should be, even though it obviously wasn't that way.
- I held on to habits that did not serve my highest good, including smoking, drinking to excess, overeating, and overspending.
- I held on to a picture of how my life should be and spent precious little time doing anything to make that picture turn into reality.
- I held on to beliefs that I wasn't good enough, that I wasn't very likable much less lovable.
- I held on to the idea that the cards were stacked against me and there was precious little I could do

about it. I felt I was at the mercy of the universe, which at times seemed harsh and unkind.
- I held onto the conviction that I could think my way through anything and gave little if any credence to the role of my soul and Divine guidance in manifesting what I wanted in my life.

To be honest with you, holding on to a hot pan might have done less damage than some of the beliefs and situations I have held on to in my life. Here's the thing: At any point in your life, at any time you are in pain, you get to look at that pain and decide whether or not you want to let go.

Now, I am not telling you that the moment you feel the pain you should "drop the pan." Truth be told, there are some cases when pain helps you to grow. The pain of self-discipline leads to ultimate joy... that is the kind of pain you want in your life. Don't be afraid of that pain; embrace it!

We all have an inner guidance system that helps us know when it's time to let go. Listen to that inner voice... the sooner you respond to it, the less pain you'll feel. The more you ignore it, the more pain you'll feel.

Now you know the key piece about how to let go. You notice the pain... feel the pain... and then decide to release it. There is something important to keep in mind here: Once you let go, pick up something else that is right for you.

If you are letting go of a relationship

- Pick up the habit of being in a kinder relationship with yourself and keeping your standards high.
- Don't make the mistake of assuming all relationships turn out the same way. Keep your heart open to forming loving, kind and compassionate relationships with others.

If you are letting go of a bad habit, such as smoking, overeating or overspending

- Take on a positive habit. You will know it's a positive habit if after you've done it, you feel proud of yourself (bad habits often feel good in the moment, but they tend to lead to regret later).
- Be around others who are making the positive choices that you want to emulate.
- Immerse yourself in reading and studying about how to form the particular positive habits you want to bring into your life.

If you are letting go of a belief that keeps you feeling less-than, unloved, or unworthy

- Take on the habit of positive self-talk. Notice whenever you are being unkind to yourself and reframe the critical language with unconditionally loving language.

- Practice saying things like "I love myself. I accept myself. I am lovable and loving" several times a day. Even if it doesn't feel genuine at first, keep repeating these words as they do have a transformative power that will make a huge impact in your life.

If you are letting go of trying to control your entire life instead of trusting Divine guidance

- Pick up the habit of affirming "I do not need to be in control of everything or know everything. I trust that my heart and soul will guide."
- Explore spiritual and consciousness-raising resources and support groups that resonate with you.

Sometimes, you might "let go" of a situation or problem in your life and then find that you have picked it back up again. Don't be upset or beat yourself up – that happens from time to time. But the process of letting go again is the same: Notice when you are holding on to something that is painful, decide whether you want to let it go, and be willing to release it. Even if you don't feel you can release it right at that moment, just begin by affirming "I am ready to release _____ in my life." By placing that simple yet sincere intention in your heart will help you find a way to let go.

Last but not least, stop thinking that letting go of something means there will be a painful void in your life. Letting go can be an enormously liberating experience, one that can and should be celebrated. Ever since that sweet little Disney princess from the Disney movie "Frozen" sang out "Let it Go! Let it Go!," we now have a powerful anthem to sing in our hearts (or aloud if you feel so inclined!!) to remind ourselves that some things are just not worth holding on to. It may be a bit corny, but I find myself humming this tune whenever I'm dragging my feet on letting go of something I know I need to release. It makes me smile, which generally will remind me of why I wanted to let go in the first place.

Letting go of unwanted things, habits, attitudes beliefs and even people is an ongoing process for anyone who wishes to grow and expand spiritually. Allowing and accepting more of who you are requires inner journey and reflection, it also sometimes involves a bit of pain and suffering, and requires loads of compassion for oneself and everyone around you. As much as possible, relax, enjoy it and celebrate the process as often as you can. Know that letting go, as children are so good at, is the key to your growth and development throughout your life.

Chapter 16 – Setting the Stage for the Formula

I believe that the real answer to any problem or situation no matter how big or small is, at the core, a spiritual one. In light of this, I want to introduce you to the chakra system before we get into the five steps of my formula.

Following is a brief description of this spiritual system for those who do not know anything about chakras. While I have studied much in this area, I do not consider myself to be an expert on all there is to know and embody about chakras. If you wish to deepen your understanding of this subject, I encourage you to check out the work of Anodea Judith, she has written a number of books which give excellent insights and guidance.

What is a Chakra?

Chakra is a Sanskrit word meaning wheel or vortex, and it refers to each of the seven energy centers of which our consciousness, our energy system, is composed. These chakras, or energy centres, function as pumps or valves, regulating the flow of energy through our energy system. The functioning of the chakras reflects decisions we make concerning how we choose to respond to conditions in our life. We open and close these valves when we decide what to think, and what to feel, and through which perceptual filter we choose to experience the world around us.

You could think of chakras as invisible, rechargeable batteries.

They are charged and recharged via contact with the stream of cosmic energy in the atmosphere in much the same way that your home is connected to a central power (electricity) source – the only difference is that this infinite energy source is free and available to all of us at all times.

Imagine this, a vertical power current rather like a fluorescent tube that runs up and down the spine, from the top of the head to the base of the spine. Think of this as your primary source of energy. The seven major chakras are in the centre of the body and are aligned with this vertical "power line."

Chakras connect our spiritual bodies to our physical one.

They regulate the flow of energy throughout the electrical network (known as meridians) which runs through the physical body. The body's electrical system resembles the wiring in a house. It allows electrical current to be sent to every part and is ready for use when needed.

Sometimes chakras become blocked because of stress, emotional or physical problems. If the body's 'energy system' becomes blocked, restricted or can not flow freely it is likely that problems will occur. The consequence of irregular energy flow may result in physical ailments and discomfort or a sense of being mentally or emotionally out of balance.

Here is a brief description of each Chakra:

Transpersonal Chakras

7. **Crown Chakra** — Represents our ability to be fully connected spiritually. Universal Identity (self-knowledge)
   Located: At the very top of the head.
   Emotional issues: Inner and outer beauty, our connection to spirituality and pure bliss.
   Demon*: Attachment
   Right: To Know

6. **Third Eye Chakra** — Represents our ability to focus upon and see the big picture. Archetypal Identity (self-reflection)
   Located: Forehead, just above and between the eyebrows.
   Emotional issues: Intuition, inner vision, imagination, wisdom and the ability to think and make decisions.
   Demon*: Illusion
   Right: To See

Egoic Chakras

5. **Throat Chakra** — Represents our ability to communicate. Creative Identity (self-expression)
   Located: Throat.
   Emotional issues: Communication, self-expression of feelings and the truth.
   Demon*: Lies
   Right: To Speak
   Letting Go Formula Step: To Aspire

4. **Heart Chakra** — Represents our ability to love. Social Identity (self-acceptance)
   Located: Center of chest just above the heart.
   Emotional issues: Love, joy and inner peace.
   Demon*: Grief
   Right: To Love
   Letting Go Formula Step: To Adapt

3. **Solar Plexus Chakra** — Represents our ability to be confident and in control of our lives. Ego Identity (self-definition)
   Located: Upper abdomen in the stomach area.
   Emotional issues: Self-worth, self-confidence, and self-esteem.
   Demon*: Shame
   Right: To Act
   Letting Go Formula Step: To Take Action

Somatic Chakras

2. **Sacral Chakra** — Represents our connection and our ability to accept others and new experiences.

Emotional Identity (self-gratification)
Located: Lower abdomen, about two inches below the belly button.
Emotional issues: Sense of abundance, well-being, pleasure and sexuality.
Demon*: Guilt
Right: To Feel
Letting Go Formula Step: To Have Acceptance

1. **Root Chakra** — Represents our foundation and feeling of being grounded. Physical Identity (self-preservation)
Located: Base of the spine in the tailbone area.
Emotional issues: Survival issues such as financial independence, money, and food.
Demon*: Fear
Right: To Be Here
Letting Go Formula Step: To Have Awareness

* *Demons of the Chakras interfere with their health and undermines their identity.*

The 7 Chakras of the Human Body

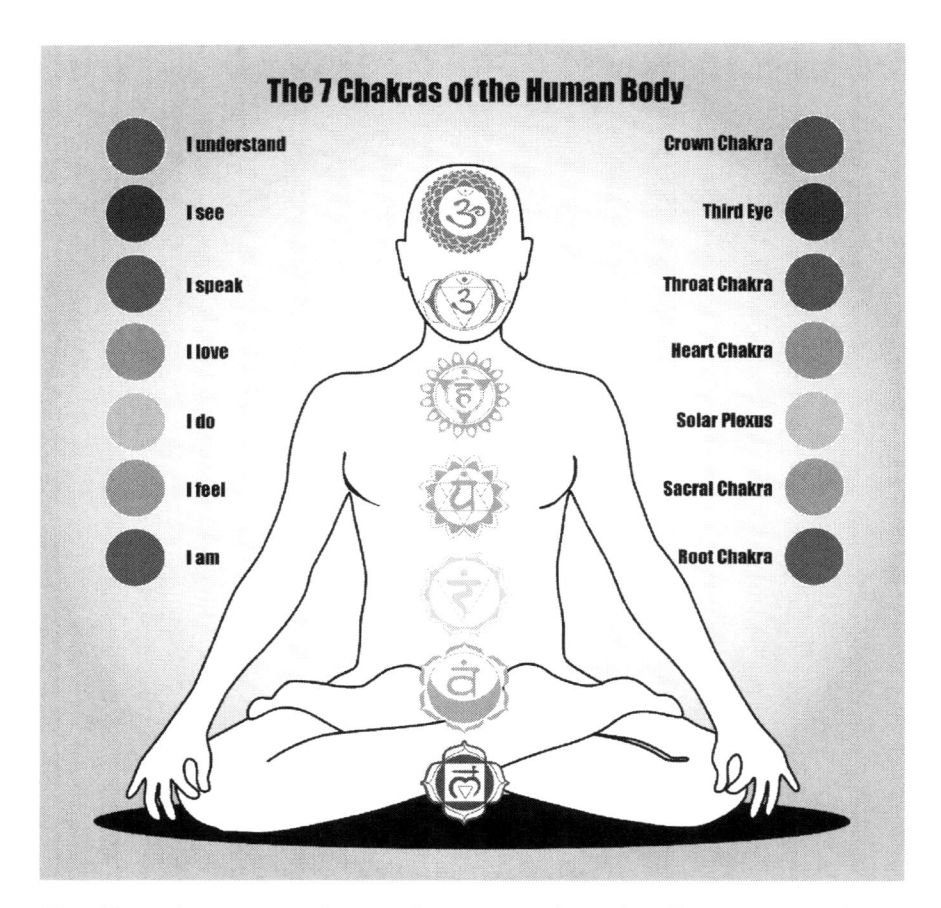

- I understand — Crown Chakra
- I see — Third Eye
- I speak — Throat Chakra
- I love — Heart Chakra
- I do — Solar Plexus
- I feel — Sacral Chakra
- I am — Root Chakra

To dive deeper and get clear on what the five parts of my formula and how to integrate them into your practice, it is important to have a sense and an ongoing relationship with your Crown and Third Eye Chakra (noted above as the Transpersonal Chakras).

As we learned above, the Crown Chakra is our energetic connection with the Divine or Source energy and the Third Eye is concerned with our inner wisdom, intuition, and perception. To make the five steps of the Letting Go

Process work for you on an ongoing basis, it is important to access and strengthen your connection to Source energy AND enhance your intuition – I believe that both of these areas are like muscles and require consistent and ongoing attention and "workouts."

My advice (and personal preference) is to have a daily meditation and journaling practice – meditation connects you with all that is and writing in a journal helps you receive your inner guidance and arrive at those "a-ha moments" which can sometimes escape our conscious awareness.

The first two stages of the Letting Go Process are rooted in your relationship with you as a body – and are connected to the "Somatic Chakras" (soma = body), and the next three stages are connected to our sense of self, in other words, the "Egoic Chakras".

It is in the realms of the "Transpersonal Chakras" where we can grow and evolve beyond the limitations of the ego and the personality. Transpersonal experiences are defined as experiences "in which the sense of identity or self extends beyond the individual or personal to encompass wider aspects of humankind, life, psyche or the cosmos."

Chapter 17 – The 5-Step Formula for Letting Go

The five-step formula to support you *letting go* to thrive in your life is:

1. Awareness
2. Acceptance
3. Action
4. Adapt
5. Aspire

First, we need to be ***aware*** – aware of where we are, what is working, what is not working, what we want to be, have and do – this is like starting off with an inventory. Next, we need to ***accept*** what is; the truth is we cannot change anything unless we *accept*. Of course, acceptance is not about labeling something as right or wrong, good or bad, nor does it mean we are going to keep it… if I accept that I have an unhealthy habit like overeating, accepting that does not mean I will continue with that pattern.

Once we have become aware and accept what is, we can then take ***action*** – this will help us take a step toward what we wish to create or experience. (So let's say in the case of having the habit of overeating, that your action is to start using smaller sized plates and eating one serving at meal times). When we take that action step, we get to have a sense of what's possible and desirable. This leads us to the fourth phase which is ***adapt*** – now we are someone different, perhaps a person who eats slower and smaller portions and feels healthy and good about taking positive steps to well-being.

These four steps help you feel like you are thriving – at this point, the fifth step starts, and we start to ***aspire*** to the next best version of us and the experience. Perhaps there is an activity you've always wanted to try but always felt too heavy or unfit to do it – start to plan and visualize doing this.

We will now dive deeper into each component separately, however, as noted above, please keep in mind that this is an organic, flowing process where each step makes way for the next. This process also keeps repeating itself in an ever-increasing way – I describe it as an upward spiral that supports you to thrive on all levels of your being!!

1. Awareness

Awareness is the first step in the formula. As you grow in self-awareness, you will better understand why you feel what you feel and why you behave the way you do. That understanding provides you the opportunity and freedom to change those things you'd like to change about yourself and create the life you want. Without fully knowing who you truly are, self-acceptance and change become impossible.

Getting clear about who you are and what you want (and why you want it), empowers you to consciously and actively translate those desires into reality. Otherwise, you'll continue to get "caught up" in your internal dramas and unknown beliefs, allowing hidden thought processes to determine your feelings and actions.

If you think about it, not understanding why you do what you do, and feel what you feel is like going through life with someone else's mind. How can you make wise decisions and choices if you don't understand why you want what you want? It's a complicated and chaotic way to live never knowing what this stranger is going to do next.

So - Who's the expert?

When we want good, reliable information, we turn to the experts. So, who are you going to turn to for information about yourself? Who's the expert?

You!!

Does a friend, a therapist, a minister, your hero, your spouse, your parents know more about you than you? They can't. You live in your skin and mind twenty-four hours a day, seven days a week, and fifty-two weeks a year. Day in and day out. No one's closer to you than you! The answers are in there, perhaps all you've needed to solve your riddles is a useful question to help you look within.

2. Acceptance

Acceptance is all about being loving and happy with who you are NOW. Some call it self-esteem, others call it self-love, but whatever you call it, you'll know when you are accepting yourself because it feels good. It's an agreement with yourself to appreciate, validate, accept and support who you are at this very moment, even those parts you'd like to change eventually.

This is important... even those parts you'd eventually like to change. Yes, you can accept (be okay with) those parts of yourself you want to change some day.

If acceptance feels so good and is so good for us, then why don't we accept ourselves? The answer is motivation. We use our lack of acceptance (punishment - because it feels bad) as motivation to get us to do, not do, be, and not be what we think we should.

Many people believe that if they accepted themselves as they are, they wouldn't change or that they wouldn't work on becoming more of who they want to be.

Typically, we judge ourselves unfavorably with the hope it will motivate us to change. We hope if we feel bad enough about ourselves, that maybe that will motivate us to change. Does this work? Sometimes… but only for the short term. Most times all it does is make us feel bad which saps the energy you could have used to make changes. It can be a vicious cycle. It works exactly counter to what you wanted to do.

So, if it doesn't work, why do we keep doing it? Because we hope it will work. And if you don't know any other way to change, what options do you have? We've been trained to believe that to change; we need first to feel bad about it. That if we're accepting and loving of that particular quality, that we won't do anything to change the situation, which is not true! You don't have to be unhappy with yourself to know and actively change those things you'd like to change about yourself. Acceptance is the very first step in the process of change.

Think of acceptance of yourself like being okay with where you live now. You may want a bigger house one day. You may dream about that new home. But there ARE advantages to residing in a smaller home if you only took the time to think about it. It is possible to be happy with the home you're in now, while still dreaming and working to make your new home a reality.

Acceptance exists at the core of your being. It is your default status. To reach this base level of acceptance, you need only remove the items lying upon the surface. To do this, you must first identify all the things you do not accept about yourself. Then, one by one, eliminate them by examining and questioning your beliefs around that issue.

- Know yourself and your beliefs
- Take a good hard look at your integrity level
- Acknowledge you are doing the best you can
- Lighten up with your value judgments
- Examine any feelings of guilt
- Understand your motivations

3. Action

The Law of Attraction teaches us that if we focus on something enough if we give it enough energy to bring it into the physical and then line up with that vibration, we can receive whatever it is we want. Sometimes, the Universe will just drop whatever it is we're looking for right in our lap. A family member will just give you their car, for example.

Sometimes, we become inspired to take some action, like walking into a store we've never been into and never even noticed, where we just happen to meet the love of our life. And sometimes we just have to wait patiently for the Universe to do its job. So, how do we know when to take action?

There's a big difference between taking action just to make something happen and taking inspired action, which is moving with the energy in motion. The key here is to recognize when you're trying to make things happen, instead of allowing the manifestations to show up in the right way for you.

When you take inspired action you:

- Get an impulse or an idea to do something, which usually comes to you naturally, easily and often at an unexpected moment.
- The action steps just make sense. You don't have to explain them; they just feel right.
- Feel energized by the action - it doesn't seem like "work." You are enjoying the process.
- Make a lot of progress very quickly and with little effort.
- Are allowing things to happen naturally. Your action is just one piece of the bigger picture.

4. Adapt

Change makes us examine our lives and to pause to gain perspective. It is possible that some changes or losses will cause us to look into the past, perhaps creating a sense of helplessness about what is now different. It can also cause us to look into the future and not understand how we might function without that part of our identity or meaning.

Throughout our daily lives, we are faced with choices. With each decision, we have a mini-loss of the other option. We also experience a gain of what we did choose. We have many gains, shifts, losses, and transitions, whether they seem huge or seemingly insignificant, throughout each day of our lives. This flexibility allows us to maintain forward movement in our lives. However, when we experience a significant loss, a subtraction that leaves us frozen, we can temporarily crumble.

The beauty of life, and all beings is that we are adaptable. We adapt continuously. We shed, and we adjust. Some losses that can leave holes in our lives, voids that could never be filled — but when we learn to accept that life is full of loss, we can hold space for it and let go of the idea that we can control it or prevent it from happening. We can learn to accept that some losses cannot be replaced, fixed, or repaired, but instead, honor it for what it meant to us.

Feelings of joy, excitement, hope and anticipation of what is yet to come can come from positive change. It can shift us forward and motivate us. Sometimes it can seem impossible to see the positive changes amidst the tragic ones. Just like the seasons, however, we keep growing, and blooming, and thriving.

Change can cause some of us to walk in place and feel stuck. It can cause some of us to walk in circles, feeling lost. But the easiest thing to do is to keep walking forward, one step at a time, even if it can sometimes take an uncomfortable amount of effort to do so. It is tougher on us to stay still. It can keep us feeling stuck and disempowered. To keep one foot in front of the other will keep you growing, learning, exploring, adapting, accepting and continuing to thrive.

5. Aspire

The last step in this formula (before starting the whole thing all over again of course 😊) is to aspire to be the next best version of YOU!! At this point, I encourage you to craft your statement of aspiration (or personal mission statement).

If "statement of aspiration" or "personal mission statement" sounds too heavy, you can call it something else! A declaration of intent. A manifesto. Your quest, on paper. A vision outline. A declaration of brilliance (or awesomeness.

I realize that this idea might sound awfully serious and binding. But it doesn't have to be. In fact, the best mission statements change, develop and evolve as you do.

The things that were important to you five years ago may no longer be applicable, and that's great as it means you are aspiring, progressing and growing. So, please don't feel like committing something to paper means you are bound to it forever. You are still the boss of you.

Another thing to keep in mind is that you don't have to complete this in a day, or even a week. It might take you some time to put together your mission statement. In fact, I believe that the more time it takes you, the better and the more in tune with you the outcome will be. Allow your mind ample space and time to percolate, nurture and blossom the ideas. Perhaps you could start with a rough outline and fill it out over the rest of the month. Make this exercise something you create time for every day.

Here's how to start:
Take a piece of paper and your favorite writing instrument (I like using a mechanical pencil). Sit somewhere comfortable and write down some questions. I like these, but they are just examples to get your creative juices flowing. There are no set rules with this step.

- I am at my best when…
- I am at my worst when…
- What do I really love to do at work?

- What do I really love to do in my personal life?
- My natural talents & gifts are…
- What are my values? What is most important to me?
- What are some goals I would like to achieve this year?
- What kind of image do I hope to project? Is it similar or dissimilar to the image I am projecting right now?
- What are my roles in life? Do I like them? Are there roles I wish for?

Allow your mind to wander around these questions (and any others you create for yourself) and jot down anything that comes up for you. It helps if you can be open-minded about this, and not limit yourself. No one else has to see this, so please feel free to be completely honest.

Another great thing to add to this piece of paper (or multiple pieces of paper!) is a selection of quotes or sayings that evoke strong feelings within you. By doing this, you will start to see patterns around what crucial to you. From here, you can pick key phrases as well as words that seem to keep coming up and blend them together to make the first draft of your personal mission statement. There are no rules: just put words together and see what develops in front of you. This is a major step into opening yourself up to thriving and claiming all that you desire and deserve.

Chapter 18 – Aligning to Thrive

When I talk about the concept of alignment, I am referring to the synching up of the physical, emotional, mental and spiritual facets of YOU.

When we allow ourselves to express fully as a spiritual, emotional and physical entity – all working in concert – all focused on the highest good; the JOY we experience, and express is INCREDIBLE. This allows for the naming and claiming of what we want, and it just feels right.

I believe that when any part of our being falls out of alignment, it is at that point where struggle and strife starts to develop and then, once started, it can be used as proof or justification of why things like "the Law of Attraction" or "ask and you will receive" do not work for you.

The teachings of Abraham-Hicks show us that it is our feelings that can guide us into a sense of alignment. The fact is – in this human experience that we are all sharing; the ultimate goal is to feel good, to experience joy, peace, and fulfillment.

> *"Hard work is not the path to Well-Being. Feeling good is the path to Well-Being. You don't create through action; you create through vibration. And*

then, your vibration calls action from you." ~ Abraham-Hicks

Some people work hard at accumulating wealth, material gain, qualifications, etc. but what I am suggesting is that we stop looking outside of ourselves for a sense of fulfillment.

We cannot always control our environment or the reactions and actions of those around us, BUT we can control our actions and reactions in our environment.

It is important to learn to trust yourself and keep and open dialogue going with yourself. At the end of the day – you are answerable to no-one else before yourself.

So, if something does not FEEL right or it does not seem to sit right in any way – that's perfectly OK. It means it is not good for you – perhaps things will change and that is OK too! But just because some form of perceived authority tells you to think or behave in a certain way, you still must check in with yourself and operate from a space of self-integrity.

It can be quite exciting when you find that you do not agree or conform with everything you see and hear around you – it allows for individual expression and development.

FEAR and GUILT are two strong forces which can throw you out of alignment and then shows up as choices and decisions that are not always based upon what is going to serve you the best, or what is really an expression of what you want.

I would invite you to ask yourself these three questions when you find yourself in a situation that does not feel supportive or nurturing to you.

- Is this good for me?
- Will this bring me closer to what I really want?
- What do I need to change?

Based upon your answers – you will be able to make the changes and choices required to bring you closer to WHO YOU REALLY ARE i.e. into alignment with yourself!

Chapter 19 – Mastering the Art of Self-Talk

Every one of us engages in self-talk. Do you find yourself saying things like, "Eek, I'm late again," or "It would be just like me to mess up this presentation!"?

Wouldn't you rather hear things like, "I did a fantastic job on that project," or "My clothes are fitting so well now that I'm exercising more!"?

Mastering the art of self-talk means you speak honestly and positively to and about yourself. When you become skilled at this, you'll feel empowered and encouraged. As a result, your days will be filled with joy and happiness, you'll work harder to achieve your goals, and you'll feel better about yourself.

Your self-talk is a powerful thing – it affects vitually everything about your life! Your self-talk influences what you believe about yourself and how you'll act (and react) in the future.

Try these techniques to help you master this life-affirming art:

- Keep it real. When you're honest, you'll feel more comfortable with yourself. If you know you could have done better on a work project, acknowledge that to yourself. Part of making progress and improving in life is being authentic with yourself about what you're doing. You can do this without being harsh.

- Avoid self-criticism. Although being honest with yourself is important, it's also equally important to do it in a supportive and informative way. Instead of saying, "I messed up," acknowledge your decision to perform to a higher standard. Tell yourself how you'll respond in the future.

- Be positive. Talking to yourself in negative or derogatory ways is self-sabotage. If you hear the same things over and over, you start to believe them. Make sure what you say to yourself is positive and self-nurturing.

- Focus on your strengths. As you listen to your inner voice throughout your day, you'll notice that you inadvertently make comments about yourself. Saying "Why did I do that? That was dumb," ... try as much as you can to put the brakes on that - it isn't very conducive to moving forward and doing your best.

- If you recognize your strengths in the situation instead – you will be compelled to go ahead and tackle the next task with gusto. You might tell yourself, "At least I thought the situation through and believed I was doing the right thing. Next time, I'll do things differently."

- Be kind to yourself. When you're talking to yourself, are you nice? Do you take care of your feelings? When you show a caring attitude toward yourself, you'll also perform better.

Here are some suggested substitutions in your self-talk:

- Instead of saying: "Nothing I do ever turns out right," try, "I am focusing on how I can succeed when I do this particular task."

- Rather than thinking: "I should have gotten up early to exercise this morning," say, "Now I'm going to do my exercise DVD" or, "I'll walk this evening right after work."

- If you were going to say, "There's nothing special about me," change it to, "Everybody has strong points and mine are…"

Can you now see how what you say to yourself influences what you believe and the choices you make in life?

To ensure that your self-talk is empowering and encouraging, practice the tips above. You have the power to create the life you want by mastering this important art.

Chapter 20 – Finding Your Inspiration

I believe two things motivate people… ***inspiration and desperation***. There are times when people are in pain, or they are hurting so much that they feel forced to do something out of desperation. By the same token, some people realize that inspiration often instigates change.

If you are struggling to find some inspiration in your life, I urge you not to give up. Seize the moment and go out and find it. I believe that even the smallest thing can give me inspiration. I get my inspiration in the strangest of places. I might see a child playing, overhear a conversation at the supermarket, or it can be as simple as a line from a movie or TV show, which just resonates and acts as a catalyst to inspire me to take action. This often happens when I was just day dreaming... you know those times when you are not paying attention to anything in particular!

You just never know when inspiration is going to come knocking at your door :)
It is always supportive to be around people who inspire you, challenge you, and who encourage you to step out of your comfort zone. After all, these are the people who are likely to give you the strength and courage to reach further than you have attempted to reach before and to aspire to be more than you thought possible.

You can notice this when you work with like-minded people; it's so much easier to blend and resonate with each other, not just mentally or intellectually, but with your heart and soul. When you're inspired, it fills you with a sense of confidence and purpose. Inspiration is a powerful force and provides a natural source of energy that will motivate you to push yourself further. These are the times when a goal or desire is actually within your reach.
On the flip side, if you have been suffering from boredom, feeling listless and tired, or just not caring about anything or anyone, then it is more than likely that you are feeling a sense of desperation to change something in your life. Inspiration can be that catalyst for change.

First and foremost, try to find something that inspires you. Be daring, challenge yourself, you may want even to try something new, something scary that pushes you outside your comfort zone. It could even be something you always wanted to try but never had the nerve or the time to do.

Find what motivates YOU – whether it is, music, dancing, singing, drawing, or even getting back to nature. No matter what it is, you will know it when you find it! Give yourself the opportunity to change, to make your life better, and to make even more of who you are.

When you feel inspiration filling you with positive energy, you'll realize that you can in fact change. When I am nervous about doing something, I just tell myself "I can do this!" Everyone is different. Focus on what you love doing and before long; your soul will start to sing out and help you reach your full potential.

Let inspiration fill your soul and allow it to motivate you – it is a lot more satisfying than desperation.

Chapter 21 – Building Your Motivation to Let Go

Motivation is a funny, complicated thing. Something that motivates one person is always different from that of another even though they may be striving for the same thing.

While people can motivate others, they can only do so to a certain degree. At the end of the day, you still have to work out a way to get yourself moving. But when everything looks bleak and all you want to do is to surrender, from where do you create the will to go on?

Begin with winning the battle in your head.

The struggle always starts in the head. One part of your mind tells you to move, work, and strive for what you are working for. The other part says that it is silliness, perhaps a waste of time. It is always easier to listen to the latter, because it is more convenient, less of a challenge, and easier to do. The former forces you to act and work. All things equal, people choose the easier way out. But this isn't always the better choice. In fact, it is pretty much never the right option.

What separates very capable people from those who are not is their ability always to make the right choices most of the time, even if these decisions are the hardest to make. They know how the game works and they try to beat it every single time. Tiring, yes, but it is also gratifying. There is always a sense of satisfaction in defeating your worst enemy - yourself.

So how do you win the battle that goes on inside your head?

Understand your thoughts and how they affect your emotions and your willpower. Negative thoughts can quickly destroy your sense of purpose. It comes in many forms - lack of self-confidence, general negativity, lack of belief in others, procrastination and so on.

Each of these has the power to convince you to throw in the towel and accept that you can't (or should not) carry on. Identifying each of your negative thoughts is the first step to overcoming a defeatist attitude.

I know, it is no simple task! It takes time before one can tune out the voice in the head that says 'give up, give in.' And sometimes, even when you have already succeeded in neutralizing your negative thoughts, it is still easy to give up at the first sign of an obstacle.

After all, it gives you a break from the perpetual struggle to achieve whatever it is you are pursuing, even for just a moment. But don't buy into that... That short period of rest can turn into days, weeks, months, years, ultimately paralyzing you from taking action and living a full life.

That's the characteristic of discouragement. It offers you immediate gratification without securing anything in return.

Try to gain positive momentum every time, instead of succumbing back into a demoralized attitude. Every time, even if that means you have to start the battle in your head all over again.

Chapter 22 – What Are Your Next Steps?

Now you have learned about the **Letting Go So You Can Thrive 5-Step Formula** and perhaps you've had a taste of what it's like to integrate the formula into your life. Perhaps you are feeling a little adrift and wondering how you can continue to transcend any limitations, blocks or obstacles to being fully all that you can be.

The key to getting YOU unstuck, and achieving your goals in your life and your business, is having a strong foundational support structure in place for you. I work with people every step of the way to make sure they move from where they are to where they wish to be with confidence and ease.

My mission is not only to help remove the roadblocks that are keeping people from the successes and achievements they wish for but also to help strategize and structure their life so that they can have fun along the way and create their best self in all aspects of their lives.

To make lasting and impactful changes in your life requires some time and effort on your part. That's why at the start of each coaching program I meet with clients (in person when possible but primarily via phone/Skype) to get the full scope of what's going on with them, their business, their relationships, their health & wellness, their goals and dreams.

It's quite common for people who have become stuck in a given situation or belief to have no idea what they want, who they want to be or what they want to do! In fact, more times than not my clients don't know where to begin (If they did, they wouldn't need me). And that's okay. As long as you know that you want to create something better for yourself, that's all that matters. We'll figure it out together!

Much love and great thriving to YOU!!
xo

About the Author

Moira Hutchison is a Mindfulness Coach, Teacher and Light Worker. It is her passion and prime directive to empower you to get fully in touch with each and every aspect of you... mind, body, spirit and emotions. Essentially what she does is help people in any way she can to allow them to find peace, joy, and calmness in personal change and challenge.

Moira works with a wide variety of clients and students from different backgrounds; mainly these are people who become aware that they have a self-limiting belief or a habit and they feel stuck and stressed. Using tools like energy work, hypnosis and coaching in the right combination for them she enables them to strengthen their internal relationship, which in turn allows them to succeed professionally, personally and in relationships.

When working with Moira, clients often comment that they resolve much more issues than what initially inspired them to seek help. For instance, someone who went to Moira for hypnotherapy for weight loss found that the relationship with her husband and children vastly improved as did her self-esteem!

Moira has studied in the fields of psychology, hypnotherapy, personal growth, self-empowerment, accounting, business organization and marketing, spirituality, metaphysics and energetic bodywork.

In her healing journey, she came to realize that she was trying to find the solutions and remedies from other people AND outside of herself. She discovered that once she learned to take responsibility and ownership for herself as a unique, sacred being that had physical, emotional, mental and spiritual needs and expression... then the real lasting healing began (and continues to this day!).

Moira firmly believes that real healing comes from within... her mission in life is to gently nudge and support you to let go of anything that no longer serves so you can actually thrive - the way you intended to!!

Printed in Great Britain
by Amazon